Leveraging Social Media to Showcase Your Design Skills

Table of Contents

1. Introduction 2

2. Understanding the Power of Social Media 3

    2.1. The Dawn of Social Media 3

    2.2. Social Media as a Game Changer 3

    2.3. The Power of Reach and Engagement 4

    2.4. The Role of Social Media in Brand Building 4

    2.5. Exploiting Social Media Features for Design Showcasing 4

    2.6. Social Media and Networking 5

    2.7. Social Media as an Avenue for Learning and Inspiration 5

3. Identifying the Right Platforms for Designers 6

    3.1. Delineation of Social Media Platforms 6

    3.2. Choosing the Right Platform 7

4. Optimizing Your Social Media Profiles 10

    4.1. Giving a Professional Touch to Your Social Media Profiles . . . 10

    4.2. Choosing the Right Username 10

    4.3. Creating a Cohesive Aesthetic 11

    4.4. Linking Your Portfolio 11

    4.5. Utilizing Highlights and Stories 11

    4.6. Tailoring Bio as per Platform Requirements 12

    4.7. Leveraging Keywords and SEO Techniques 12

5. Creating a Stellar Digital Portfolio 13

    5.1. Building Blocks of a Digital Portfolio 13

    5.2. Effective Presentation of Your Designs 14

    5.3. Making Your Portfolio Stand Out 14

    5.4. Updates and Maintenance 15

    5.5. Beyond Your Portfolio - Testimonials and
Recommendations 15

6. Upscaling Your Designs for Social Media Viewing 16

6.1. Preparing your designs for the digital landscape 16

6.2. Choosing the right resolution and DPI 17

6.3. Incorporating optimization techniques 18

6.4. Accommodating for various screen sizes 18

6.5. Testing and adjusting 19

7. Leveraging Instagram and Pinterest for Design Exposure 20

7.1. Using Instagram for Design Exposure 20

7.2. Leveraging Pinterest for Design Exposure 21

7.3. Combining Instagram and Pinterest for Maximum Impact . 22

8. Engaging with Your Online Community 24

8.1. Understanding the Importance of Engagement 24

8.2. Engagement Strategies: From Passive to Active Engagement . 24

8.3. Creating and Sharing Content That Resonates 25

8.4. Leveraging Engaging Features on Social Media Platforms . . . 25

8.5. The Art of Responding Positively 26

8.6. Growing Through Collaboration and Partnerships 26

8.7. Consistency is the Key 26

8.8. Evaluate and Adapt 27

9. Driving Traffic with SEO and Hashtags 28

9.1. Harnessing the Power of SEO 28

9.2. Amplifying with Hashtags 29

9.3. Tracking Success and Refining Your Strategy 30

10. Measuring Success: Analytics for Designers 31

10.1. Understanding the Basics of Social Media Analytics 31

10.2. Leveraging Advanced Analytics Tools 32

10.3. Turning Insights Into Actions 32

10.4. Devising an Analytical Routine 33

11. Staying Trendy: Adapting to Social Media Changes 34

11.1. Identifying Trend Shifts 34

11.2. Adapting Your Creative Process 35

11.3. Updating Your Social Media Strategy 35

11.4. Continuous Learning and Upskilling 36

11.5. Staying Ahead with Analytics and SEO 36

Design is not just what it looks like and feels like.
Design is how it works.

Chapter 1. Introduction

In the digital age, where innovation and creativity are as esteemed as traditional knowledge, sprucing up your talents online can make all the difference. We're excited to unveil our Special Report titled "Leveraging Social Media to Showcase Your Design Skills." This seminal guide provides both rookies and veterans with smart strategies to effectively broadcast their design prowess for maximum exposure. Through a vibrant blend of expert advice, best practices, case studies, and action points, we're about to help you transform your social media platforms into a captivating portfolio that speaks volumes about your capabilities. Ready to dazzle the digital world with your designs? Buckle up, because this outstanding report is your ticket to standing out in the design crowd!

Chapter 2. Understanding the Power of Social Media

Social media has truly revolutionized the way we communicate, share information, and market our skills and talents. When harnessed correctly, it has the power to greatly amplify your reach and impact as a designer. This fact can no longer be ignored in our hyper-connected, digital age.

2.1. The Dawn of Social Media

It's important to reflect upon the inception and growth of social media to better understand its power. The advent of social media platforms in the early 21st century introduced a new communication paradigm. Such digital platforms transformed the way individuals, businesses, and movements express themselves and engage with the world at large. In essence, social media burgeoned into not just a space for interpersonal connection but also a powerful tool for professional advancement.

2.2. Social Media as a Game Changer

Today, the importance of social media in showcasing your talents, especially in creative fields like design, cannot be understated. With various platforms to choose from, each with its own set of unique features and user demographics, social media offers individuals a global platform to showcase their work and connect with prospective clients, collaborators, or employers. In the realm of design, social media can serve as a dynamic, interactive portfolio, bringing together images, video, text, and even augmented and virtual reality elements to bring your designs to life for a global audience.

2.3. The Power of Reach and Engagement

The power of social media lies in its reach and the ability to engage with a diverse audience. Platforms such as Facebook, Instagram, Twitter, and LinkedIn have millions, even billions, of active users worldwide. This means that an eye-catching design posted on one of these platforms has the potential for unrivaled visibility and reach. Crucially, this reach is not just passive. Audiences on social media can interact directly with your work—liking, commenting, sharing, tagging, saving, and even purchasing. This engagement is invaluable; it gives designers immediate feedback on their work, opens up possibilities for collaboration or commission, and builds community around their brand.

2.4. The Role of Social Media in Brand Building

In addition to showcasing individual design pieces, social media enables designers to present and build their brand effectively. Via your social media profiles and the content you share, you can display your unique design style, your areas of expertise, your values, and your personality. This helps potential clients or employers to understand not just what you can do, but who you are as a designer.

2.5. Exploiting Social Media Features for Design Showcasing

Moreover, each social media platform comes laden with an array of features that can powerfully showcase your design work. High-resolution photo and video posting, Stories, Reels, IGTV, Pinterest boards, Facebook albums, Twitter threads, LinkedIn posts and documents—each offers unique possibilities for effectively showcasing your designs, your process, and your achievements.

2.6. Social Media and Networking

When it comes to networking and relationship-building, social media is a boon. The platforms enable designers to follow and interact with fellow creatives, industry influencers and potential clients. Direct messaging features provide a opportunity for initiating contact, discussing collaborations or job opportunities. Hashtags allow for increased visibility, helping your designs reach audiences searching for specific content.

2.7. Social Media as an Avenue for Learning and Inspiration

Lastly, for designers, social media is an immense source of inspiration and learning. Other designers' work, design trends, tutorials, tips, industry news, design memes—there's a wealth of content accessible through these platforms that can inform and enrich your design practice.

Given this expanse of possibility that social media platforms offer, understanding and effectively leveraging their power is key for any designer looking to enhance their online presence and reach. As we delve further into this report, we shall unpack strategies and best practices for doing just that, one platform at a time.

Chapter 3. Identifying the Right Platforms for Designers

As seasoned designers and novices alike navigate the waters of the digital age, one of the primary points of interest inevitably falls upon social media platforms. These online mediums are not just about scrolling through indecipherable gibberish or losing yourselves in the enchanting world of memes and dog videos, although we cannot blatantly deny the guilty pleasures they do offer. Instead, they prod at a boundless realm teeming with possibilities waiting to be explored and harnessed. Ideally, they can act as levels of a launchpad to elevation, provided we know which platforms to lean on for showcasing our design skills and how to utilize them to the hilt. In this elaborate narrative, we will dive deep into this topic to help you pinpoint the digital terrains where you sway and sway exceptionally well.

3.1. Delineation of Social Media Platforms

First off, let's meticulously sift through the cornucopia of social media platforms at our disposal. They each have their unique inclinations, communities, and method of content digestion, which effectively categorizes their use.

Facebook: Once the poster child of the social media world, Facebook continues to hold a massive crowd. However, it is more generalist in nature and may not specifically cater to the needs of designers unless leveraged meticulously.

Instagram: This platform arguably holds the throne for visual creativity at present. It is a paradise for photographers, graphic designers, fashion designers - virtually anyone dabbling in the stream of aesthetics - displaying their work to a vast, discerning crowd.

LinkedIn: A formal social platform majorly reserved for professional networking and corporate establishments. It is a powerful platform if you aim at commissioning work, networking with like-minded professionals, and showcasing your design acumen in a professional light.

Pinterest: Unrivaled for its image-centric approach, Pinterest is a hub of inspiration and marvellous ideas. It's where designers can create visually stunning boards to showcase their work and draw users to their websites or other social profiles.

Behance and Dribbble: These platforms are designer-specific, sporting portfolios from a global community of designers. They extend beyond just social media, providing a dedicated space to host portfolios, engage in peer critique, follow inspiring designers, and get noticed by potential clients.

Tumblr: A microblogging site that can effectively support visual media, texts, and links. If your design forte is towards the unconventional, and you wish to blog about it, Tumblr with its varied demographics could be your answer.

Twitter: A text-heavy platform that demands brevity and wit, Twitter can yield dividends if a designer wishes to discuss the field, follow industry leaders, and build a strong network rather than just portfolio showcasing.

3.2. Choosing the Right Platform

Once we have dissected the world of social media platforms, it's time to zero in on the ones that resonate with your design aesthetic, audience, and personal preferences.

Here's what the selection process can involve:

Understand your Target Demographic: Identifying the age range, profession, interests, and behavioral patterns of your target audience is crucial. You must know where your crowd hangs out, what kind of content they consume, and how they interact with it. These insights will help you decide which platforms to concentrate on.

Determine the Scope of your Design Discipline: Each design discipline has its niches within social media. For instance, Instagram and Pinterest are prime territories for visual designers, while LinkedIn serves the corporate design world well. Behance and Dribbble are more suited to product or UX/UI designers, and Tumblr can beautifully embolden the illustrative side of design work.

Identify your Communication Style: Your style of communication is a mirror reflection of your personal brand. Some designers excel in communicating through images, some through words, and some through audio-visual content. Decide your forte and choose the platform accordingly.

Ease of Use and Maintenance: Every social media platform requires consistent effort and attention. Strike a balance between your enthusiasm for managing social media and the actual time or resources you have at hand.

The Goal of Your Social Media Presence: Be clear about what your primary goal is. Are you on social media primarily to showcase your portfolio, to network with other designers, or to communicate directly with customers? Your goal will help guide your decision.

By carefully examining this multitude of factors, preparation will meet opportunity on the digital field. Remember, every platform has potential, but your best bet is where your bread and butter lie. That platform will be your megaphone, broadcasting your brilliance and design skills to the world, laying down the red bricks on your road to social media success. And as you traverse this route, bear in mind that your platform choice is not a one-time, irreversible decision. The digital world evolves at a blistering pace, and so should you. Explore, experiment, be fluid, and continually redefine your social media strategy based on your successes and lessons learned.

Let's dive deeper into how to optimize and effectively use a few popular platforms in the forthcoming chapters. Hold on tight because our journey into the vibrant world of social media with design at its core has only just begun.

Chapter 4. Optimizing Your Social Media Profiles

In the journey to amplify your design skills and showcase your portfolio to the world, optimizing your social media profiles is the critical first step. With so many social media platforms functioning as a resilient and multifaceted marketplace for ideas, projects, and images, it's more vital than ever to create an appealing, professional, and representative profile that is tailored to your brand essence. This chapter serves as a comprehensive guide to optimizing your social media profiles, incorporating thorough explanations, insightful tips, and practical steps that designers can employ to enhance their online presence.

4.1. Giving a Professional Touch to Your Social Media Profiles

To create an impact in a highly visual domain such as design, your social media profiles should uphold a sense of professionalism. This involves polishing all facets of your profile, including your profile picture and bio. Opt for a clear, high-resolution profile picture where you look professional and approachable. Your bio should encapsulate your brand's vision, your unique selling proposition, and a touch of your personality. Remember, the bio is a wonderful opportunity to put forth your values and aspirations. Use each word to your advantage and incorporate a CTA (Call to Action) inviting profile viewers to scroll down, view your portfolio, or visit your website or blog.

4.2. Choosing the Right Username

The username, or handle, is much like a billboard on a busy highway, which could either be easily forgettable, or one that creates a lasting impression. To ensure the latter, select a unique, memorable, and search-friendly username that reflects your name or brand. It should be consistent across all platforms to establish uniformity, recognition, and ease of search for followers.

4.3. Creating a Cohesive Aesthetic

As a designer, you have the power to tell your brand's story through images. Therefore, your feed needs to embody a consistent aesthetic that aligns with your brand. This could be a specific color scheme, layout style, or a combination. This consistency communicates a strong brand identity while providing a visual treat to profile visitors.

4.4. Linking Your Portfolio

To direct traffic to your portfolio, include a clickable link in your bio. This could lead to your professional website, blog, or a simplified mobile portfolio. A cohesive, well-organized website conveys professionalism and sets the tone for your work ethic and style.

4.5. Utilizing Highlights and Stories

On platforms like Instagram, leverage the 'Highlights' feature to showcase your best projects or a behind-the-scenes look at your design process. These become permanent fixtures on your profile, serving as handy previews to what followers might expect in your feed.

4.6. Tailoring Bio as per Platform Requirements

Each platform harbors different demographics and fortes. For instance, LinkedIn is ideal for showcasing your professional accomplishments and full resume, while Instagram might demand more creativity and personality. Dedicate some time to understand each platform's dynamics and culture to tailor your biography and content accordingly.

4.7. Leveraging Keywords and SEO Techniques

In the digital realm, visibility is contingent on search engine rankings. So, incorporating relevant keywords, common search phrases related to design, and SEO techniques into your profile would make it easier for people to discover your work.

In summary, profile optimization is an amalgamation of creativity, strategy, and a deep comprehension of your personal brand. Create an inviting and impressive online storefront that compels visitors to explore more of your work. The ultimate goal is to cultivate an online profile that not only showcases your work but also resonates with your unique personality and design philosophy. A well-optimized social media profile acts as a powerful promotional tool that can significantly amplify your reach, helping you secure fruitful collaborations, projects, and recognition in the design world.

Chapter 5. Creating a Stellar Digital Portfolio

In this digital age, your design work is now more than ever an available canvas for the world to see and appreciate. As a designer, your digital portfolio remains one of the most crucial aspects of your online presence. It acts as a bridge that connects you with potential clients, collaborators, and employers. Indeed, your portfolio shapes first impressions and communicates your personal brand, design philosophy, creativity, and technical skill.

5.1. Building Blocks of a Digital Portfolio

To begin, one must focus on the essential elements of a digital portfolio. A successful portfolio is more than just a collection of your work; it's a showcase of your growth, dedication, and personality as a designer.

The first thing to consider is the user interface (UI). Ensure your portfolio site is navigable and intuitive. Pay meticulous attention to the design, color schemes, and typography, they should echo your personal design style. Make the navigation as straightforward as possible, but don't be afraid to add a dash of creativity into your site's navigation. Consider including a 'Home', 'Portfolio', 'About Me', and 'Contact' page for easy navigation.

Next is the content; your selected works. Aim to feature a range of projects that covers the broader spectrum of your capabilities without overwhelming visitors with too much information. Aim for depth rather than breadth. Present your primary, most successful projects with detailed case studies, describing your roles, responsibilities, tools, processes, outcomes, and, if possible, client feedback.

5.2. Effective Presentation of Your Designs

The way you furnish your portfolio with your work can greatly affect your audience's perception. Each project representation should contain an intriguing story about your design process. Include the brief you were given, your initial ideas, sketches or drafts, refinements, and finally, the finished product. Providing a narrative not only showcases your final designs but also sheds light on your journey and thought process, something prospective clients or employers would be interested in.

When using images in your portfolio, ensure they are of high quality. Poor, pixelated images may misrepresent the quality of your work. Consider using a mixture of images, such as full-layout shots, detailed close-ups, and the design in context (for example, how a website looks on a laptop or mobile device).

5.3. Making Your Portfolio Stand Out

With a sea of designers vying for attention, how do you make your digital portfolio stand out? Start with an exceptional About Me section. It's your opportunity to tell your story, your design journey, your philosophy, and your passion. Write in a conversational tone, and remember, this is your chance to build a connection with your audience.

Another opportunity to stand out is by creating a custom domain name that either uses your name or a unique identifier that aligns with your brand. This step not only helps with brand consistency but also aids in search engine optimization (SEO).

5.4. Updates and Maintenance

The digital world moves briskly, and so should your portfolio. Keep your portfolio current with recent works, technology, and design trends. Regularly updating shows you are an active participant in your field.

Also, conduct regular audit sessions, during which you examine and improve your portfolio's user experience. This activity should also encompass the validation of external links, and keeping your contact information up to date. It's also an opportunity to weed out older work examples that no longer represent your skill level.

5.5. Beyond Your Portfolio - Testimonials and Recommendations

Lastly, consider testimonials or recommendations. You might have created the most brilliant designs, but words of endorsement from clients, colleagues, or mentors will further boost your credibility. People are often more inclined to trust peer reviews, which serve as powerful tools that validate your skills and expertise.

By following these guidelines, you can sculpt a digital portfolio that doesn't just display your work, but tells your entire design story. It will not only attract prospective clients or employers but will also allow you to carry out self-assessments and track your growth as a designer in the digital arena. Your portfolio shouldn't merely exist; it should emanate your essence, narrate your story, and position you as the go-to professional in your field. The creation of a stellar digital portfolio is not just an endeavor but a journey, on which you convert your creative visions into tangible realities and invite the world to admire your artistic prowess.

Chapter 6. Upscaling Your Designs for Social Media Viewing

In the realm of design and visual artwork, the preeminence of image clarity and quality cannot be overstated. We're all familiar with the saying that 'a picture is worth a thousand words,' and in the digital landscape, this couldn't be more relevant. Social media acts as both a platform and magnifying glass for your designs. It's a showcase where your style and creativity meet the global arts community. However, the platform itself can pose quite a challenge. Different platforms have individual criteria in terms of picture quality and dimensions, making the task of displaying your work accurately a fine art in itself. This chapter will guide you through actionable techniques and considerations for upscaling your designs for social media viewing, keeping them as vibrant and engaging on screens of various sizes as they are up close.

6.1. Preparing your designs for the digital landscape

Creating outstanding digital designs is only half of the battle. The other half is successfully transforming these for digital consumption while retaining the striking appeal of the original. To do this, we will delve into the world of digital image formats, social media platform specifications, and image editing tools.

Digital image formats vary in terms of quality, size, and compression. The most commonly used image formats on the internet are JPEG, PNG, and GIF. JPEG images are perfect for complex graphics and photographs due to their ability to handle a wide array of colors. PNG files provide lossless compression, making them ideal for text, line art, or when transparency is needed. GIFs are best suited for animations.

When preparing your designs for social media, you must also be mindful of the standard dimensions that each platform accepts and displays. Remember, using the wrong dimensions can result in skewed, stretched, or pixelated designs – certainly a nightmare scenario for any designer!

Several image editing tools are available at your disposal, such as Adobe Photoshop, GIMP, or Canva, which can streamline the process of upscaling your designs. These tools allow for automatic resizing, image compression, and other adjustments to match your design with the platform's specifications.

6.2. Choosing the right resolution and DPI

A crucial aspect of upscaling your designs for viewing on social media is understanding resolution and dots per inch (DPI). The resolution of your image plays a significant role in its displayed quality. Too low, and your image will look pixelated; too high, and it might be too large for the platform or slow down page loading times.

Understanding DPI is essential mainly for print designers who are transitioning their work to digital platforms. A higher DPI means more detailed output in print but does not necessarily translate to better quality on digital platforms, as screen display relies on pixels.

So, how do you balance resolution and DPI? Generally, for digital platforms, a DPI of 72 is sufficient, while the resolution should fulfill the specific platform's guidelines. An astute rule of thumb for resolving is to keep your images in the 1080p to 4K spectrum, ideal for both mobile and desktop viewing.

6.3. Incorporating optimization techniques

While resolution and DPI are vital, there's so much more to the digital display of your designs. Optimization involves adjusting the file size, format, and dimensions without jeopardizing the image quality.

You can use a litany of tools to compress image files effectively. Tools like Photoshop allow you to 'Save for Web' which automatically optimizes the image. Online tools such as TinyPNG or Compressor.io compress images without significant quality loss.

Beyond just manual optimization, there are also ways to automate the process for scaling, giving your workflow a much-needed efficiency boost. Platforms like Cloudinary or imgix provide APIs to do this, resizing and optimizing images on-the-go.

6.4. Accommodating for various screen sizes

Another critical consideration is screen sizes. With users viewing social media on various devices from smartphones to desktop computers, your design must be legible and visually appealing across all devices.

The concept of responsive design comes into play here. Initially a hot topic in web design, the idea of making your design 'respond' to the size of the screen it's being viewed on is increasingly relevant in the age of multi-device browsing. Designing with a variation of screen sizes in mind ensures your core ideas won't get lost in translation because of differing display sizes.

Lastly, remember that each social media platform will have its own guidelines and recommendations for uploading images. Platforms like Instagram and Pinterest, known for their visual slant, have specifically tailored uploading instructions to help you showcase your work in the best light possible.

6.5. Testing and adjusting

Once you have upscaled your designs and followed all the guidelines, the last but equally important step is testing. The design might look perfect on your screen, but it's imperative to check how it appears on various devices and internet speeds. This process is also an excellent chance to assess viewer engagement and adjust accordingly.

Through this chapter, you will have gleamed crucial knowledge about adapting your work for the digital sphere. Ensuring your designs maintain their quality and impact across numerous digital platforms can prove challenging, but it's one hurdle that, once conquered, can push your designs from great to phenomenal. As with many things, practice and consistency will make progress easier, and soon, the digital upscaling of your designs will become second nature.

Chapter 7. Leveraging Instagram and Pinterest for Design Exposure

Instagram and Pinterest, two of the most visually-oriented platforms in the world of social media, bear immense potential for designers looking to nurture and flaunt their skills. With their inherent focus on aesthetics and imagery, an encapsulating design portfolio on these platforms can catch the eye of countless onlookers and elevate your brand visibility like never before. Here, we introduce you to comprehensive strategies to leverage these platforms for maximum design exposure.

7.1. Using Instagram for Design Exposure

As one of the most popular social media platforms, Instagram offers a vast audience base and a seamless interface centered around presenting visual content. Thus, it stands out as an excellent platform for designers looking to grow their visibility.

Let's look at the steps you should take to put your design talents on the Instagram map:

1. **Consistency is Key**: Maintain a consistent aesthetic across your posts. This could be a similar color palette, design style, or theme. It serves to underscore your individuality and aids in brand recognition.

2. **Hashtags**: Harness the power of hashtags. They tie communities together on Instagram and give an enormous boost to your content visibility. The right hashtag can bring your design to thousands of people who might never have found your work

otherwise.

3. **Engage with Other Users**: Instagram is not just about posting; it's also about building relationships. Engage with followers, respond to comments, and don't hesitate to connect with other designers. This can lead to collaborations, referrals, and an expanded reach overall.

4. **Stories and Reels**: Instagram Stories and Reels offer additional avenues to showcase your designs. You could give behind-the-scenes glimpses of your design process or share quick tutorials to engage your audience in a more informal way.

7.2. Leveraging Pinterest for Design Exposure

As a platform harboring creative ideas, Pinterest has become a virtual mood-board generator. For designers, it provides an opportunity to share designs with a group of people who are actively seeking visual inspiration.

Consider these tactics to present your work effectively:

1. **Custom Board Covers**: Pinterest lets you create custom covers for your boards. Utilize this feature to present your boards in a cohesive way that aligns with your design aesthetic.

2. **Descriptive Pins**: When uploading a design, make sure to include keyword-sensitive descriptions. These will make your designs more discoverable to people who are searching for those keywords.

3. **Engage With Communities**: Similar to Instagram, engaging with others on Pinterest is fundamental. Comment on other's pins, join group boards, and follow relevant users.

4. **Promoted Pins**: Consider tapping into Promoted Pins, where you pay to have your pin appear in certain locations. This could be a

worthwhile investment if your main goal is to increase visibility of your designs to a wider audience.

7.3. Combining Instagram and Pinterest for Maximum Impact

The key to exerting maximum design exposure lies in combining the strengths of Instagram and Pinterest. While Instagram can help create a sense of intimacy with behind-the-scenes insights and real-time interactions, Pinterest offers a more organized and categorically segregated platform that's perfect for showcasing distinctive design projects.

To interlink the utilities of both platforms, consider these steps:

1. **Cross-Promote Your Platforms**: Use each platform to guide users towards the other. For instance, include your Instagram handle in your Pinterest bio, and vice versa.

2. **Repurpose Content**: Reuse content to maintain consistency in your aesthetic across the different platforms. Nevertheless, remember to tailor the description and hashtags to suit the specific platform you are posting on.

3. **Leverage User-Generated Content**: Pitch contests or challenges that encourage followers to contribute their own creations or interpretations. Not only does this yield a treasure trove of content, but it also facilitates deeper engagement and fosters a sense of community among your followers.

4. **Measure and Adapt**: Use the analytics provided by both platforms to gauge your performance. Assess which type of content resonates best with your audience and constantly iterate your strategy based on this feedback.

Effectively leveraging Instagram and Pinterest is much more than just broadcasting your designs. It involves exploiting the unique features of these platforms, proactively engaging with their communities and continuously fine-tuning your approach based on the analytics. By mastering these methodologies, you can metamorphose these platforms into a powerhouse for showcasing your designs and capturing the attention of a vast spectrum of audience.

Chapter 8. Engaging with Your Online Community

In the dazzling world of digital design, engaging with your online community is not an option; it is a necessity, a priceless conduit to build relationships, increase visibility, and garner support for your work. This chapter offers proven strategies to facilitate effective engagement with your online community through the judicious use of social media.

8.1. Understanding the Importance of Engagement

At first glance, social media may seem a cluttered space, an arena for mindless chatter. However, on closer inspection, a different picture emerges - one of a global stage offering unlimited opportunities for designers to reveal their talents, create impact, and form consequential connections.

Engaging with your online community is more than posting content; it's about nurturing relationships, creating dialogues, and converging around shared passions and interests. By investing time and effort in engagement, you secure a two-fold benefit; you enhance your brand's visibility and create a strong, loyal community.

8.2. Engagement Strategies: From Passive to Active Engagement

Your approach to community engagement should be a hearty blend of passive and active strategies. Passive engagement requires observing, listening, understanding trends and interests, gauging user responses, and determining how best to align your work with community preferences. Active engagement, on the other hand, demands active participation, regular posting, replying to comments, and reaching out to users.

Empathy, respect, and friendliness should underscore your active engagement initiatives. Remember, your aim should not be to attain the highest number of comments, but to create meaningful connections that progressively expand your creative horizons.

8.3. Creating and Sharing Content That Resonates

Mastering the art of tailoring content to suit your target audience is key to engaging your online community. This requires a clear understanding of your target demographic, their needs, preferences, and expectations. Once you have this insight, construct your posts around these parameters, ensuring they resonate with your audience and spur engagement.

It's worth noting that engagement-oriented content may not always be strictly about design. Behind-the-scenes peeks, a tour of your workspace, or sharing what inspires you can make your followers feel invested in your journey, fostering stronger bonds.

8.4. Leveraging Engaging Features on Social Media Platforms

Almost all social media platforms offer native features that enhance interaction. From Q&A sessions on Instagram Live to design polls on Twitter, strategically use these features to invite community participation and gain feedback. Further, live streaming and video content are exceptional ways to capture attention and stimulate online interaction.

8.5. The Art of Responding Positively

Listening is as crucial as talking. Always respond to comments and queries; it signifies that you value followers' opinions. An ignored comment may come across as disrespectful, which can tarnish your reputation.

Moreover, the digital space can be unpredictable, and negative comments are a reality. If addressed correctly, such situations can be turned around. Embrace negative feedback with grace and professionalism, and view these situations as an opportunity to reinforce your brand values.

8.6. Growing Through Collaboration and Partnerships

Collaboration and partnerships with other designers or design-centric brands on social platforms can help you engage with a larger audience. This can be through joint live sessions, collaborative projects, or shared content. Such partnerships are beneficial for everyone involved, leading to cross-promotion and shared growth.

Social media contests can also emerge as a successful strategy to drive engagement. They often lead to significant escalations in visibility and interaction, plus they fuel community spirit.

8.7. Consistency is the Key

Consistency in social media participation fortifies your online presence, which in turn stimulates engagement. It builds anticipation among your followers and establishes a sense of familiarity with your brand. Regular activity on your chosen platforms increases the probability of your content being seen and engaged with by your audience.

At the same time, consistency doesn't mean you saturate your followers with content. Find a balance, creating and sharing high-quality posts that offer value, education, inspiration, and motivation.

8.8. Evaluate and Adapt

In conclusion, as the digital landscape continues to evolve, so too should your engagement strategies. Analytics can provide useful insights into what works and what doesn't for your brand. Based on these insights, review and recalibrate your strategies regularly. Befriending change and mastering adaptability will keep you in good stead in this dynamic environment, paving the way for an ever-growing, engaged, and loyal community.

Chapter 9. Driving Traffic with SEO and Hashtags

Overlooking the power of Search Engine Optimization (SEO) and hashtags in driving traffic to showcase your design work can be detrimental, as you may miss out on getting your creations in front of a vast audience. The proper utilization of these two tools can significantly enhance your visibility, steering numerous prospective clients, collaborators, and fans towards your work.

9.1. Harnessing the Power of SEO

SEO, in essence, is the process of structurally framing your digital content to improve its visibility on search engines. To generate heavy, repeated footfall on your portfolio, the two facets of SEO we need to pay attention to are on-page and off-page SEO.

On-Page SEO crucially involves the optimization of your content and site structure. Start by conducting keyword research. Use tools like Google Keyword Planner or Moz's Keyword Explorer to find high-volume, relevant search terms related to your design skills. Pepper these keywords throughout your posts, captions, meta-descriptions, alt texts, and URLs modestly, without appearing forced or artificial. Equally important is to employ descriptive, catchy titles and headers, utilizing your high-ranking keywords when applicable. In addition, ensure your website is well-structured, loading smoothly and quickly. Failure to do so might have potential viewers bounce off quickly, negatively affecting your bounce rate and SEO rankings.

Off-Page SEO, on the other hand, mainly focuses on building trust and authority. One effective way to build credibility is through link building. This can be through having external websites linking back to your content (backlinks), or internally linking your own content (internal links). The former can be achieved by guest blogging, collaborations, or simply creating captivating content that people naturally want to link. Internal links not only enhance user experience, but also guide search engine bots, establishing the importance hierarchy of your site's content.

9.2. Amplifying with Hashtags

After mastering the basics of SEO, it's time to flex our social media muscles by delving into the world of hashtags. Prevalent on platforms such as Instagram, Twitter, and Pinterest, hashtags are integral mechanisms that can bolster your content's discoverability.

To reap their benefits, you need to create an effective #hashtag strategy. Begin with broad, high-volume hashtags, like #graphicdesign or #architecture, depending on your specific design niche. These tags improve your chances of being discovered by a sizable, general audience.

However, don't neglect niche hashtags, as they can help you reach a more targeted audience, typically comprised of industry specialists and enthusiasts. For example, if you're a designer focused on eco-friendly concepts, using a specific tag like #greenarchitecture or #sustainabledesign could attract an audience specifically interested in those areas.

In addition, you can create your own brand-specific hashtags. This can simply be your brand name, a tagline, or anything that uniquely represents your work. With consistency, these personalized tags can amplify your brand's visibility and cultivate a community around your content.

Remember to respect the platforms' guidelines when it comes to using hashtags. Instagram, for instance, allows a maximum of 30 hashtags per post. However, studies suggest that 9-11 tags garner the most engagements.

9.3. Tracking Success and Refining Your Strategy

A crucial part of your SEO and hashtag strategy is to continually evaluate your success and refine your approach. For this, analytics tools like Google Analytics and Instagram Insights are invaluable. They allow you to understand which keywords and tags are generating traffic, audience engagement, and conversions.

Start with tracking your website traffic and social media engagements. Then, delve deeper into which keywords or hashtags churn the most interactions. Was it the general, high-traffic keywords and hashtags, or the more niche ones? Knowing this can guide you towards more efficient keyword and hashtag strategies.

Ultimately, it's about understanding your audience and catering to their interests. This constantly evolving process of testing, learning, and adjusting is the secret recipe to maximizing your design showcase potential through SEO and hashtags.

In conclusion, a potent blend of well-executed SEO strategies and a snappy hashtag game will significantly elevate your visibility on search engines and social media alike. By incorporating these attributes into your strategy, you will unlock a wider audience reach and greater engagement, ensuring your design work rockets to the attention it truly deserves.

Chapter 10. Measuring Success: Analytics for Designers

Once your social media strategies and design sharing plans are underway, it is crucial to continuously monitor and measure their effectiveness to ensure you are moving towards achieving your goals. This chapter aims to elucidate the significance of analytics in determining the success of your endeavors, and provides a comprehensive overview of utilizing both basic and advanced measurements in order to maximize your visibility, engagement, and influence as a designer.

10.1. Understanding the Basics of Social Media Analytics

Social media analytics is the practice of gathering data from your social media platforms and analyzing it for beneficial insights. These could range from identifying the kinds of content that resonate best with your audience, discerning the best times to post, or tracking follower growth. Social media platforms boast an ocean of data that, when properly analyzed, can provide deeper insights into your audience, their behavior, and how they perceive your design work.

The first step towards leveraging analytics to one's advantage is to understand the key performance indicators (KPIs) that matter most. Some versatile KPIs for designers can include engagement, reach, impressions, follower growth, and traffic.

1. Engagement: This metric refers to how people are interacting with your content, and can be measured through likes, comments, shares, or saves.

2. Reach: This means the number of unique users who viewed your content.

3. Impressions: This involves the total number of times your content was displayed, including multiple views by a single user.

4. Follower Growth: This stands for the increase in your follower count over time.

5. Traffic: This is an indicator of how many people are visiting your website or portfolio link via your social media profiles.

10.2. Leveraging Advanced Analytics Tools

After grasping the basics of social media analytics and determining the KPIs that resonate with your objectives, you can delve into more advanced features and tools. These can give you more detailed, specific insights that the basic metrics, though beneficial, might overlook. There are a plethora of analytics tools available on the internet- both standalone tools, as well as built-in features on each social media platform.

Free tools such as Google Analytics can be incredibly potent when connected to your portfolio website. They can provide vital data on demographics, behaviors, devices used by users while visiting your site, and the channels that drive more traffic. Other tools, like Sprout Social or Buffer, combine the analytics from multiple social media platforms and present them in a digestible format, saving time and simplifying the data analysis process.

10.3. Turning Insights Into Actions

Measurement is futile without action. Utilize the insights derived from your analysis constructively to fine-tune your strategies. If your designs receive more engagement during a specific time of the day or days of the week, try posting more frequently during those times. If a particular style of your designs is gaining traction, focus on producing more of such content.

It's crucial to embrace an iterative process. Test fresh formats, content styles, and engagement strategies, then measure their success via analytics. Tweak your plans based on these learnings and repeat the process.

10.4. Devising an Analytical Routine

Designers are inherently busy and juggling various tasks at once. Hence, it is helpful to establish a routine for checking your analytics. You don't need to analyze your metrics daily, as fluctuations occur all the time and looking daily can lead to premature and inaccurate conclusions. Instead, choose a specific day of the week or month to fully delve into and interpret your analytics, then make strategic plans based on those insights. A methodical, recurrent examination of your metrics will ensure that your social media strategies evolve and improve over time.

Achieving social media success isn't an overnight feat; instead, it's a journey that involves constant monitoring, analysis, adjustment, and learning. By measuring your efforts and refining your strategies using analytics, you set yourself on the path towards a bigger online presence, more engagement, and ultimately, increased recognition and respect as a designer. The power of analytics enables you to step up your game and make more informed, strategic decisions to showcase your design skills effectively in the digital world.

Chapter 11. Staying Trendy: Adapting to Social Media Changes

In the ever-evolving landscape of design, change is the only constant. Much like fashion, design trends morph, blend and often sprout from existing foundations to create fresh perspectives. We thrive in dynamic environments and, to maintain relevance and continue growth in this sphere, we must keep our finger firmly on the pulse of the latest trends. This chapter dives into pivotal strategies for staying trendy and responsive to shifts in the social media design landscape.

11.1. Identifying Trend Shifts

The first step in staying contemporary involves the ability to identify emerging social trends. Regularly reviewing popular culture blogs, news sites and other forms of media can assist in this regard. However, honing in on social media platforms themselves often provides the most direct insight into user preferences.

- Social media influencers: Following key influencers within your niche can keep you informed about current happenings and budding trends.

- Hashtag tracking: A key to unlocking social trends lies within monitoring hashtags. Popular hashtags can often indicate trending styles or burgeoning ideas.

- Competitor analysis: Regularly scrutinize your competitors' social media presence. Any successful changes they implement can inspire fresh updates in your design strategy.

11.2. Adapting Your Creative Process

Proactive trend tracking allows for immediate identification of popular creative elements emerging within the design field. Incorporating these elements into your design itself serves to imbue your designs with a zeitgeist, a spirit of the times.

Remember, however, not to lose sight of your unique style. The goal is not to blend into the trend, but to layer your designs with contemporary elements that amplify your distinctiveness. Strike a balance between what's popular and your individual artistic voice.

11.3. Updating Your Social Media Strategy

Keeping up with changes on social media platforms themselves is equally essential. Each social media platform tends to evolve separately, with unique updates and changes. Staying on top of these tweaks can allow you to leverage new features for broader exposure and better engagement.

For instance, Instagram regularly introduces new features like Instagram Reels or Instagram Guides which designers can use to showcase their work in different, engaging ways. Being aware of, and experimenting with new features as soon as they are available increases your visibility, enabling potential clients and other designers to discover your work more readily.

11.4. Continuous Learning and Upskilling

In the vein of continuous adaptation, investing time in learning new tools, software, and methods can turn potential challenges in the trend landscape into opportunities for growth. Online resources and tutorials, webinars, or design festivals provide rich avenues for learning.

11.5. Staying Ahead with Analytics and SEO

Having a firm grasp of your analytics is a vital aspect of trend adaptation. Analytics can reveal what content resonates with your audience, the best posting times for engagement, revealing client behavior, and more. Equally important is understanding SEO and the application of keywords to promote discovery of your designs.

Staying trendy isn't merely reacting to change - it's anticipating shifts and proactively implementing strategies to stay at the forefront. Remember, maintaining an adaptable mindset, continuously learning, and staying plugged into social dynamics will ensure you flourish in the fluid, fast-paced world of design.

In the end, keeping a vigilant eye on trends, suitably adapting your strategies, and effectively leveraging SEO and analytics will allow you to entwine your design skills' brilliance with the continually transforming social media landscape. Stay relevant, stay updated, and watch as your design presence evolves, much like the social media landscape you're navigating.